How to use this coloring book:

Rule #1: Have fun. This book is meant to make you smile, laugh, & have a good time with friends. Don't take it seriously! It's all meant for quirky good fun!

Rule #2: You can scan and print individual page images for personal use so you can color an image more than once, or to share with friends. You're allowed to scan images for coloring digitally too.

Rule #3: Be creative and give finished works away as rediculous gifts. To aid with cutting, use a ruler and a sharp knife to remove pages.

Rule #4: Please do not post uncolored pages on-line or sell any images for profit, colored or not. You are encouraged to show off your colored images as much as you want though, as well as show photos or video for book review purposes! Keep in mind these images are for adults only when you do.

Rule #5: Refer to Rule #1 & enjoy!

Copyright
2019 SledgePainter
All Rights Reserved

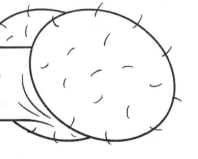

Cut VS Uncut

Peenie Sushi

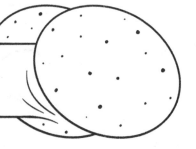

Hard 4 U Valentine

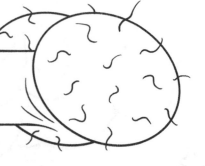

Shrinkage

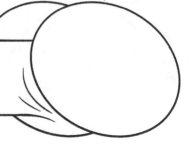

Ninja Peen

Rub 'N Tug Troubles

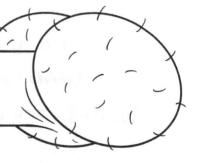

Rubbers

Dick Pics

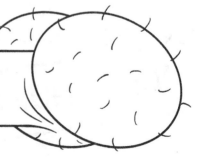

Dick Pics

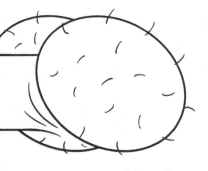

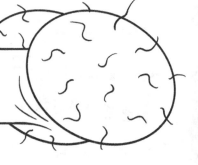

Bag 'O Dicks

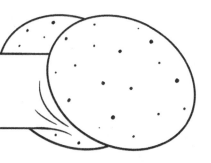

Cock Fight

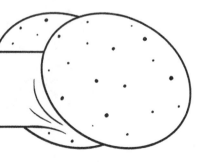

Magic Rainbow Showers

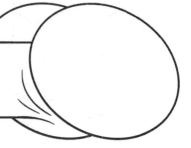

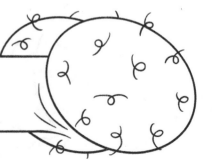

 Sperm Whale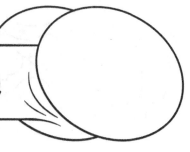

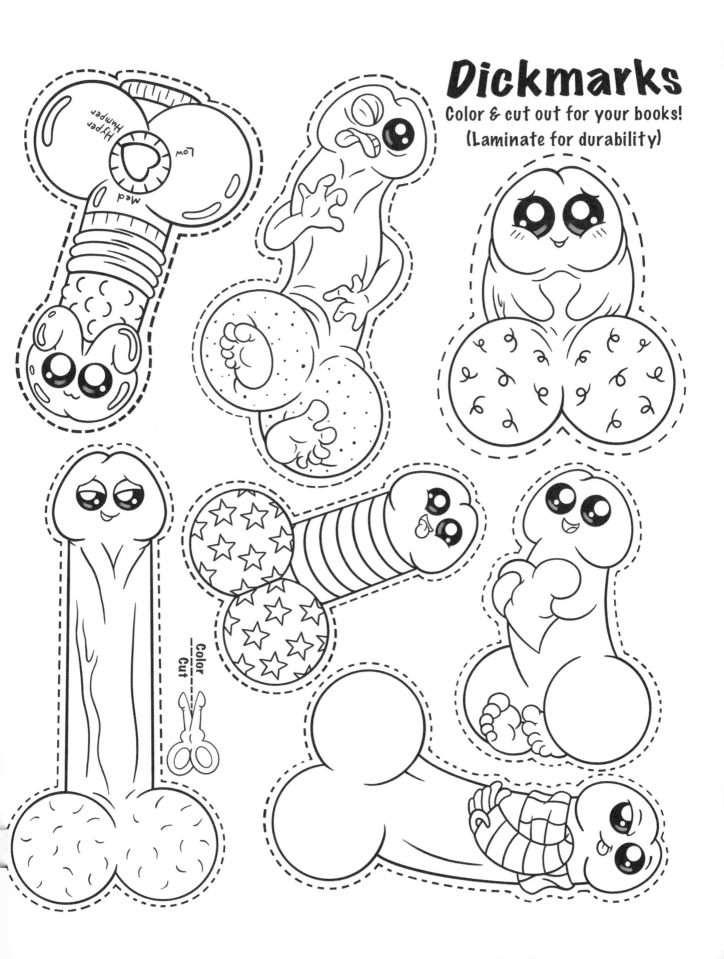